FERGUSON
CAREER BIOGRAPHIES

HALLE
BERRY

Actor

James Robert Parish

Ferguson
An imprint of ☑®Facts On File

Halle Berry: Actor

Copyright © 2005 by Facts On File, Inc.

Ferguson
An imprint of Facts On File, Inc.
132 West 31st Street
New York NY 10001

Library of Congress Cataloging-in-Publication Data
Parish, James Robert.
    Halle Berry : actor / by James Robert Parish.
      p. cm
    Includes bibliographical references and index.
    ISBN 0-8160-5827-X (alk. paper)
   1. Berry, Halle. 2. Motion picture actors and actresses—United States—Biography. 3. African American motion picture actors and actresses—Biography. I. Title.
    PN2287.B4377P37 2004
    791.4302'8'092—dc22   2004003954

Ferguson books are available at special discounts when purchased in bulk quantities for businesses, associations, institutions, or sales promotions. Please call our Special Sales Department in New York at (212) 967-8800 or (800) 322-8755.

You can find Ferguson on the World Wide Web at http://www.fergpubco.com

Text design by David Strelecky

Pages 95–112 adapted from *Ferguson's Encyclopedia of Careers and Vocational Guidance, Twelfth Edition*

Printed in the United States of America

MP Hermitage 10 9 8 7 6 5 4 3 2 1

This book is printed on acid-free paper.

CONTENTS

1 An American Beauty   **1**

2 A Modest Beginning   **7**

3 Breaking into Show Business   **21**

4 Building a Hollywood Name   **33**

5 A Traumatic New Beginning   **49**

6 Inspired by Dorothy Dandridge   **61**

7 Claiming Her Oscar   **77**

Time Line   **91**

How to Become an Actor   **95**

To Learn More about Actors   **109**

To Learn More about Halle Berry   **113**

Index   **117**

1

AN AMERICAN
BEAUTY

On March 24, 2002, at the 74th Annual Academy Awards, Halle Berry won the Oscar for Best Actress for her performance in the dramatic film *Monster's Ball*. Not only had Halle emerged victorious over her impressive acting competition—Judi Dench, Nicole Kidman, Sissy Spacek, and Renée Zellweger—but the 35-year-old was the first African American actress to ever win the Best Actress Oscar.

In her highly emotional Oscar acceptance speech, the much surprised and very pleased Berry said of her acting idols and peers: "This moment is so much bigger than me. . . . And it's for every nameless, faceless woman of color that now has a chance because this door tonight has been opened. Thank you. I'm so honored."

Halle Berry was the first African American to win the Academy Award for Best Actress. She won for her performance in the film Monster's Ball. *(Photofest)*

More Than Just a Pretty Face

For Halle Berry the road to winning the coveted Academy Award was long and arduous, not only professionally, but also personally. A child of a biracial marriage (her mother is white and her father, who is deceased, was black) who was raised by one parent after her abusive father left the family, Halle coped with an extremely difficult childhood. She witnessed continual physical and emotional abuse in her home as a child. She also endured similar types of emotionally and physically abusive situations in some of her own adult romantic relationships.

In addition, when Halle was in her early twenties she discovered she was suffering from diabetes, a serious physical condition that requires constant medical monitoring to keep her health stabilized. Once she became a recognized show business personality, Halle's experiences with abuse and diabetes led her to become a spokesperson for both of these important causes.

Professional Challenges

On a professional level, Halle had to overcome many challenges in her career, which she began as a beauty pageant participant. As a youngster, Halle decided to identify with and be part of the black community rather than straddle two ethnic worlds. The biracial, light-skinned Halle experienced much prejudice and discrimination in her efforts to rise within the acting field. As she struggled to break into acting in the late 1980s and early 1990s, there were still relatively few nonstereotypical and significant acting roles for people of color, especially women, in American television or film. These fields continued to be dominated by white actors. Halle had to compete in an extremely limited marketplace for an opportunity to display her talents.

Ironically, one of the greatest obstacles in Halle's career growth was her spectacular beauty. In describing the actor in a 1995 *New York Times* article, Jill Gerston wrote of Halle's "exquisite cheekbones," "flawless café au lait skin," "eyes like two huge dark caramels," and "wrists so narrow they look as if they could almost fit through the hole of a doughnut." Halle is considered one of the world's most stunning women. *People* magazine included her in one of its famous "50 Most Beautiful People" issues, and she is an international spokesperson for Revlon Cosmetics. But for many years, agents felt that no one as pretty as Halle could possess the acting skills needed for major dramatic roles. This is a preconception that Halle still faces today, even after receiving her Academy Award.

With so many odds working against her, it is all the more remarkable that Halle Berry has accomplished so much in her life. Like many other biracial celebrities (for example, golfer Tiger Woods; singers Christina Aguilera,

Alicia Keys, and Mariah Carey; NBA star Jason Kidd; newscaster Ann Curry; and actors Vin Diesel and Keanu Reeves), Halle has overcome prejudice and emerged a champion in her chosen career.

2

A MODEST BEGINNING

Halle Maria Berry was born August 14, 1966, at Cleveland City Hospital in Cleveland, Ohio. (It was the same facility where African American star Dorothy Dandridge—an important role model in Halle's life—had been born in 1922.) Halle (which rhymes with "Sally") was named after a then-popular Cleveland department store. Berry's mother had been shopping at Halle Brothers and, while examining an array of beautiful handbags at the emporium, decided, "That's what I'm going to name my child."

Halle's mother, Judith Hawkins, was born in Liverpool, England, and had immigrated to the United States with her parents when she was six. She grew up in a suburb of Cleveland. Judith became a nurse specializing in psychiatric cases and worked at the local Veterans Administration Hospital. There she met an ex-soldier, an African American man named Jerome Berry, who was employed

7

at the institution as an orderly. The couple fell in love and were wed in the early 1960s. Judith's parents disapproved of the racially mixed marriage and disowned their daughter, while Jerome's relatives also were not pleased by his marriage to a white woman.

In 1964 the Berrys became parents when their daughter Heidi was born, followed, two years later, by Halle. The family went through difficult financial times, a situation made harder by their being snubbed and ridiculed for being an ethnically mixed household. Adding to their problems was Jerome's alcoholism. When he had too much to drink, he turned physically abusive. "He battered my mother," Halle recalled. Whenever Heidi tried to intervene to protect their mom, Jerome would turn his fury on his older child. Unlike the more assertive Heidi, Halle managed to stay out of her father's way: "He never hit me. . . . I felt a lot of guilt. When my sister saw him hitting my mother, she would jump in and get hit, but I would run and hide." (At the time Halle was growing up, very little was known or discussed about domestic violence—known as the "quiet crime." There were no counseling agencies or support groups, as there are today, to help stop cycles of abuse.)

When Halle was four, Mrs. Berry finally put an end to the ongoing domestic violence by demanding a divorce and insisting that her husband leave their house. Mother and daughters breathed great sighs of relief when they were

Halle and her mother, Judith, at the 2002 Academy Awards
(Photofest)

free of Jerome's unending tyranny. But when Halle was 10 years old, her mother chose to reconcile with her ex-husband. She hoped that he had finally mended his ways and that the four of them could, once again, be a real family. Before long, however, Jerome had fallen back into his violent behavior and began beating Mrs. Berry and Heidi again. Of her dad's reappearance in her life in 1976 and her hope that this time things would be different, Halle has said, "He was not the image I had made my daddy out to be. If I had lived with him any longer that year, I know I would have turned out to be a very different kind of person."

Soon thereafter Jerome abandoned his family once and for all. Halle never saw him again. To help Halle cope with her father's second leaving, Mrs. Berry sent her shy, introspective younger child to be counseled by a psychologist, a process the future celebrity would continue throughout the years.

Years later, when Halle had become famous, Jerome would try to reestablish ties with her, but she was too upset about the past to agree to meet him. The 68-year-old man died in January 2003 of complications from Parkinson's disease. Halle did not attend her father's funeral.

New Beginnings

With Mr. Berry permanently gone from the family, the hardworking Mrs. Berry left the black inner-city neighborhood in Cleveland where she and her children lived. They moved to Oakwood Village, an all-white Cleveland suburb that boasted a good school system. Whereas Judith Berry had been the odd person out in their black neighborhood, now her two girls suddenly experienced racial prejudice from their predominantly white schoolmates. Halle recalled that during this period she frequently found a box of Oreo cookies stuffed into her mailbox. At the time she thought, perhaps, she had a secret admirer. Only later did she realize the cruelty of the "gift," which was a racial slur implying that, like the famous cookie, Halle was black on the outside and white on the inside. Another time, a third-grade classmate insisted to Halle that her mother could not be her real parent because Mrs. Berry was white and Halle was black. The taunting youngster insisted that Halle must be adopted.

Just as Mrs. Berry successfully took care of her family's financial needs, she also helped her children deal with the many difficulties brought on by their biracial background. She worked hard to help build Halle's self-esteem after witnessing her father's abuse and the young girl's enduring racial discrimination at school. Said Halle in later years of her mother, "She always instilled in me that you are good, you are smart, you are beautiful, you are capable of doing whatever it is you want to do." One day Judith sat Halle down in front of a mirror and said, "Look at yourself. What do you see when you look at your skin?" Halle replied, "Brown." Judith then asked, "What color do you see when you look at my skin?" The girl answered, "White." The mother then explained, "That's right: You're black and I'm white; but that doesn't mean I'm not your mother, that I don't love you. You are a black little girl."

Thanks to her mother's counseling, Halle decided then and there to regard herself as part of the black community. As she would acknowledge later, "I'm discriminated against like a black woman, as if I were 100 percent African American, so that's what I feel I am."

Forging a Fresh Identity

Another great role model for Halle was her fifth-grade teacher, Yvonne Nichols Sims. In the mostly white school, Sims was a strong black woman who, Halle says, helped her to "find my way" in life. According to Berry, "She was the first person other than my mother to help me understand what being black was all about and what my struggle would be." Sims organized an after-school club for African American students to teach them about their cultural heritage by taking them on field trips to museums, art galleries, and so forth, so they could better understand and appreciate their rich ethnic background. The experiences engineered by Sims did a great deal to teach Halle about her black roots. (Coincidentally, Sims transferred to

Bedford High School as a guidance counselor at about the same time that Halle started classes there. The instructor continued to mentor the student, and the two have remained good friends.)

As Halle passed through the grades and reached Bedford High School, she compensated for her insecurities and shyness by being an overachiever in both academics and extracurricular activities. In her younger scholastic years, Halle had been a class monitor. Now in high school, the charismatic, pretty young woman expanded her goals. She was accepted on the cheerleading squad, became an honor society member, and, among several other achievements, was made editor of the school newspaper. Halle's rule of thumb was, "If there was an organization, I wanted to be the head of it. I wanted the best grades. I wanted to be the best of everything." The fact that she encountered racial bias all along the way only made her more determined to succeed in her goals. She reasoned of her white classmates, "I thought if I made the honor society they would know I was as smart as they were; if I ran the paper I'd control what's in the paper and make it diverse; if I'm a cheerleader, I'm going to be the captain."

One of Berry's most trying challenges in high school occurred when she was chosen junior class prom queen. Once selected, she was accused of having won the crown unfairly. According to Halle, "They weren't about to have a black prom queen, so they accused me of stuffing the ballot box." As she detailed further, "When it came to academics, I was always an A student and they were comfortable with that. But when it came to being the queen that was something different. And so they decided there would be a co-queen. Me and this white, blond, blue-eyed, all-American girl."

Halle found the incident "devastating." She explained, "It made me feel like I wasn't beautiful, that they don't see *us* [black people] as being beautiful." In reaction to the traumatic situation, Berry almost did not attend the prom. However, her mother convinced her to make an appearance to prove that her classmates' bias could not control the situation. So, Halle arrived at the dance with her date, the son of the school's white principal.

As a result of the prom queen election controversy, Halle lost interest in school activities. Now, with a chip on her shoulder, she could not wait to graduate high school and show her peers that, "I'm going to be somebody, and one day you're going to want to remember that you knew me because I'm going to go out and do something fabulous." At the time, she thought she might like to be an actor, and for her senior project she did scenes from the play *The Effect of Gamma Rays on Man-in-the-Moon Marigolds.* (As a youngster Halle had dreamed of one day starring in a new production of one of her favorite movies, 1939's *The Wizard of Oz*.) Her mother was supportive of this artistic ambition, but offered her younger girl some practical advice: "That's a nice dream, hon, and if one day you get the opportunity go for it. But in the meantime you need to go to college. The reality is, for a black woman, you're going to need education."

Beauty Pageants

In the months before Halle graduated from high school in 1984, her boyfriend at the time entered Berry's yearbook photo in the Miss Teen Ohio beauty pageant—unbeknownst to her. To Halle's amazement, she was chosen as Miss Cuyahoga County in the local runoff. She then became a finalist on the state level and, eventually, won the title of Miss Teen Ohio. This led to Halle competing in the Miss Teen All-American Pageant. She not only claimed her state's title, but went on to win the national pageant, becoming Miss Teen All-American 1985.

In 1986 she won the title Miss Ohio and qualified to compete in the Miss USA pageant. In the Miss USA competition, she finished in second place. However, she accepted an offer from comedic superstar Bob Hope to join his USO troupe making a three-week goodwill tour, where she had the chance to entertain U.S. troops in seven countries around the world.

Halle poses for the camera during the Miss USA competition in 1986. (Landov)

In 1987 Halle, as a Miss USA runner-up, was qualified to compete in the Miss World pageant held that year in Hong Kong. Although she lost the top rankings, she came in third, and was noted as "best dressed."

Although competing in these contests did give Halle the satisfaction of "proving" her worth to her former schoolmates, she did not enter the stressful and competitive world of beauty pageants just for the ego boost. As she made clear later, "We were very middle-class people. Not upper middle. Not lower middle. And I knew that my mother couldn't afford to flat-out send me or my sister to college. So my only hope was through scholarships and grants."

As such, Halle matriculated at Cleveland's Cuyahoga Community College. At the two-year institution she majored in broadcast journalism, thinking she might become an investigative reporter. This career ambition fizzled after her summer internship at a local TV station. On this job she was sent out with a senior correspondent to interview people involved in newsworthy stories. One of her initial assignments was to question a family whose inner-city home had been destroyed in a fire. In asking the victims about their recent plight, Halle became visibly upset. She later said, "I so lost my composure that it upset the family. I didn't have the skin for the job."

Having abandoned her journalism ambitions, Halle switched to acting classes at school. However, she soon decided continuing at college was not for her.

Coping in the Windy City

During her beauty pageant days Halle had met Kay Mitchell, a Miss USA judge. Mitchell was a talent agent in Chicago and suggested that Berry relocate to that city to try her luck in the modeling field.

Halle quickly found that the life of a struggling model in the big city was hardly glamorous. At first she shared a tiny apartment with about a dozen other professional hopefuls. Often her only meal of the day was the free snacks that local bars served during happy hour. Soon this cramped lifestyle became unworkable. Berry moved out to share a small apartment with another would-be model and friend. Later, while Berry was out of town on a modeling assignment in Milwaukee, her roommate moved out without notice. When Halle returned to Chicago she found that she owed $1,300 in rent and had no way to pay it. Unsure of what to do, she asked her mother for financial assistance. Her mother practiced tough love by refusing assistance, saying, "Now you're seeing what it's like in the real world." According to Halle, "When she said no, my world came crashing down."

The tense situation between mother and daughter grew worse when Halle, determined to put together a proper model's portfolio, asked her mother to help pay the $500 fee. Again, Mrs. Berry said no, both because she could not afford the sum at the time and to teach her daughter to be truly independent. The situation worsened between the two women and, for nearly a year thereafter, they did not speak to one another. Eventually, Halle appreciated her mother's constructive motivation: "What seemed like a really terrible thing at the moment was probably the best thing she could have ever done for me."

Meanwhile, Halle struggled to get new modeling assignments. At 5 feet, 6 inches she was relatively short for a runway model. In addition, Halle's options at the time were limited because she is an ethnic minority. She was persistent, however, and she eventually found some print ad work, especially in department store layouts for Lord & Taylor and Marshall Field's.

By then Halle was growing restless with the world of modeling, especially when she realized she could not reach the top of her profession. She simply was not tall enough, and the discrimination she faced because of her skin color prevented her from achieving her goals. So she began taking acting classes. Before long she caught the attention of New York–based talent manager Vincent Cirrincione. He suggested she move to Manhattan to pursue modeling and acting, and Halle readily agreed.

3

BREAKING INTO SHOW BUSINESS

When Halle Berry first lived in New York City, she stayed at the apartment of Vincent Cirrincione and his wife, who became her mentors and good friends. Halle continued to pursue her acting ambitions. Determined to break away altogether from the modeling field, Berry took the dramatic step of changing her curly long hair into a close-cropped style. This went against the fashion of the time for African American models and Cirrincione was upset that his client had literally cut off her chances for a modeling career. Nevertheless, he pushed to get Halle auditions in the acting field. She tried out for a role on the daytime soap opera *Days of Our Lives*. That bid failed, as did her efforts to win a part in a potential new version of the old TV series *Charlie's Angels*. While Berry did not succeed in that project (which failed to materialize anyway), the veteran producer of that series, Aaron Spelling, encouraged Halle to continue in her chosen craft. At this point in her struggling efforts to break into the acting world, Halle was especially grateful for Spelling's kindness.

The Beauty Curse

It was during this period of unsuccessful auditions and little money that Halle realized her sensational looks were both a blessing and a curse. As she analyzed later, "Beauty can be used as a tool to draw people in. But, once you're in, you've got to be able to do something. I don't think I'm bad looking, and I know my looks have made a difference in some situations. But I also see a lot of people around me who are much more beautiful than I am." On another occasion, she explained this hurdle she faced because of her striking good looks: "When you're a model they think you're stupid and they think, 'Oh, you're beautiful, so you want to be in movies but you have no talent.'"

Despite the career obstacles, a determined Berry—and her equally persistent agent—continued to hunt for acting assignments. Halle's breakthrough came in the shape of *Living Dolls*, a TV sitcom that debuted on the ABC-TV network on September 26, 1989. In ironic typecasting, she was selected to play one of four teenage models who were guided by the head of a small Manhattan modeling agency. Halle played Emily, a serious girl who intends to use her modeling income to pay for medical school. Although Halle felt that her character was a "token" ethnic figure and that the screenwriters did not know how to write for a minority character, she took the job since she needed the work and acting experience.

As a model, Halle learned that her good looks were a blessing and a curse. She would soon prove that she was much more than just a pretty face.
(Photofest)

The half-hour television series was not well received by the critics or the public. Howard Rosenberg (*Los Angeles Times*) said, "*Living Dolls* is bad enough when it tries to be funny, even worse when it tries not to be funny. As for the latter, it doesn't have to try." After only 13 episodes, the program was canceled.

Diagnosing a Serious Problem

During the hectic weeks of shooting *Living Dolls*, Halle was under a great deal of stress. One day she collapsed on the set and was rushed to the hospital. She was diagnosed as being in a diabetic coma. Diabetes is a disease that causes the body not to produce sufficient amounts of insulin, a hormone that is needed for the body to function properly. After the medical team revived Halle, she learned the facts of her severe medical condition: "The doctors told me that all of the stress I'd been under probably brought the diabetes out early. Otherwise, it might not have surfaced until I was 50 or 60."

At first Berry was terrified by the serious diagnosis. "All I heard was [having to take medical] shots every day and that I could lose my eyesight and my legs. I was scared to death." Once she had calmed down, she learned that she had type II diabetes, the most common form, which, if properly monitored, can be kept under reasonable control.

However, being in a high-stress occupation, Halle ignored some of the symptoms of her disease, such as feeling sleepy and having little energy. By ignoring or denying these symptoms, Halle put herself into potential danger. But she had a sharp wake-up call a few years later when she temporarily lost the mobility of her right leg due to her diabetes. As a result, she changed her diet positively and exercised regularly to combat her illness. She also learned to meditate to combat recurring bouts of stress. As she explained further, "I need three square meals a day. I eat lots of vegetables and make my own juices, always have some fruit and avoid sugar and fried foods."

Later, as Halle's career took off and her workday grew even busier, she installed a gym at home. With the help of a personal trainer, she still keeps herself in appropriate physical shape for a diabetes sufferer. She also became involved with the Juvenile Diabetes Foundation and has worked with that organization and other such groups to bring this often overlooked disease to the attention of the young public.

Spike Lee

During 1990–91, as Halle restabilized her body, she managed to get some small acting assignments. She had guest spots on such TV series as *A Different World* and *Amen*. She performed in a few music videos. She was seen as Debby Porter in four segments of the nighttime soap opera *Knots Landing*.

Also at this time, acclaimed African American filmmaker Spike Lee was casting a new picture, *Jungle Fever* (1991), which he had written and planned to direct. It dealt with an upscale young, married black architect (played by Wesley Snipes) who falls in love with an office temp secretary (played by Annabella Sciorra), a young Italian woman. When Halle heard about this controversial film about a doomed interracial love affair, she managed to get an audition for a supporting role. At first Lee thought Halle would be good in the small part of Vera and asked her to test for that role.

However, Halle had greater acting ambitions. She was far more intrigued by the bigger role of a drug-addicted prostitute. After much begging, Lee agreed to let her try out for the downbeat role. Even after he finally casted her in the part, he had second thoughts. He called Halle to tell her the bad news: He was giving the part to another performer. She spent the next hour on the phone begging him to reconsider, insisting, "Spike, give me a chance, give me a chance, and I will prove that I can do this." Eventually, the director gave in to her impressive bid for this dramatic opportunity.

As most actors do when faced with a challenging role, Halle went through elaborate preparations for this gritty performance. She temporarily lived on the street and did not shower for days. Accompanied by an undercover cop, she visited an actual drug house and observed how addicted prostitutes acted in real life. She was also tutored and befriended in her acting preparations by Samuel L. Jackson, the veteran performer who would play her on-screen boyfriend.

The R-rated *Jungle Fever* grossed $32 million in domestic distribution, which made the controversial film a hit.

As part of an impressive cast that included many established actors, Halle had to fight for screen time. Although her performance was convincing, even gaining her some praise from movie critics, this hard-won role did not prove to be the big career break she had anticipated. A few years later, however, after Halle had gained screen fame, moviegoers would look back in amazement that the performer who had played the drug-addicted prostitute in *Jungle Fever* was none other than Halle Berry.

Searching for Love

During the making of *Jungle Fever*, Halle reportedly began a relationship with fellow actor Wesley Snipes. When it ended, she fell into an emotional funk. In this period, she also dated singer Christopher Williams and basketball star Charles Oakley, as well as other non-celebrities. In retrospect, Berry has admitted that her romantic relationships during this time were generally not very healthy. As she detailed, "I always picked guys who needed to be rescued. I would baby them and take care of them instead of being an equal and a partner. When I came into their lives, they needed somebody to help them and to get them through a rough time. But once they got through that rough time, they'd split. . . . I was the one who always ended up getting hurt in the process."

Perhaps Halle's worst dating experience was her association with a man who was physically abusive toward her. (To this day, out of respect for the love they once shared, she has refused to name him publicly.) One time, this individual hit her so severely on the ear that she lost 80 percent of the hearing in her left ear. As a result, she had to buy a hearing aid. However, she was so self-conscious that she refused to wear the instrument. Immediately thereafter, Berry ended her relationship with this dangerous boyfriend, having learned from her mother's experience with her father that such abusive behavior generally does not stop, no matter how often the other person promises to change.

Moving On

From the heavy drama of *Jungle Fever*, Halle went into the lightweight screen comedy *Strictly Business* (1991). She was cast as Natalie, the brainy, beautiful show business hopeful who captures the attention of a rising black business executive (played by Joseph C. Phillips). The latter, a whiz at work but awkward on the social scene, relies on a conniving mailroom clerk (played by Tommy Davidson) to help him win Natalie's attention. Two days into the shoot, director Kevin Hooks had the unpleasant task of telling Berry that she was dismissed from the cast. The producers had decided that it was a cliché to have a very light-skinned black performer as the much-desired leading lady. Instead, they wanted to use an actor with darker skin. Two weeks later the filmmakers had another change of heart, and Halle was reinstated in her key role. When the movie debuted in November 1991, Hal Hinson of the *Washington Post* rated the film a "tepid comedy" and one in which the female characters are treated like "baubles." The film did very poorly at the box office.

Of more significance was *The Last Boy Scout* (1991), a big-budget action thriller. Halle plays the girlfriend of a pro football star (played by Damon Wayans) who hires a former secret service agent (played by Bruce Willis) to watch over her. Halle's role was flashy but small. Nevertheless, as with all her acting assignments, she put a great deal of effort into giving her character dimension and authenticity. However, when the filmmakers requested she do a nude love scene in the film, she refused; a body double was used for the more revealing camera moments. A violent film, *The Last Boy Scout* was dismissed by many moviegoers as mindless. The film did prove useful to Halle's later career, however, as she became good friends with the film's producer, Joel Silver, who would use her in several other screen projects.

Halle's next acting assignment was the 1992 film *Boomerang*, starring Eddie Murphy and Robin Givens. Murphy used the film to try and bring back the popularity he experienced in the 1980s. In the film, Halle plays the sweet and gentle assistant of his high-powered boss, played by Givens.

While the mediocre *Boomerang* did little to restore Murphy's popularity, Halle received highly positive reviews for her winning performance in a relatively sappy role. *Variety* labeled her the "only naturalistic character in a cast of caricatures," while the *Los Angeles Times* enthused, "Halle Berry is awfully appealing as the girl everyone wants to bring home to mother." Most favorable was the trade paper *Hollywood Reporter,* which offered this endorsement: "Halle Berry's star keeps getting bigger and brighter. Her appeal is up there with Murphy's, and her ability to change gears on a dime will win the audience over."

Finding Mr. Right

As Halle continued the Hollywood scramble to stay in the limelight, she unexpectedly found a new romance. In early 1992 Halle was being interviewed by a reporter who mentioned that he was a friend of Atlanta Braves' outfielder David Justice. The reporter said that the ballplayer had requested Halle's autographed photo. Halle was aware of the professional baseball player, who had been named Rookie of the Year in 1990. She had seen him recently in a televised celebrity baseball game on MTV. She provided her autographed photo and added her home phone number beneath her signature.

A few days later the 26-year-old sports star phoned Halle and they talked for several hours. Next, he invited her to Atlanta to watch him play baseball and then go out for dinner. She agreed. The couple quickly discovered that they had a lot in common. Both had been raised by single mothers who were nurses. (Mrs. Justice lived in Cincinnati, Ohio.) David, who had a high IQ, had skipped several grades in school. He had attended Thomas More College in Kentucky, but had dropped out when the Atlanta Braves drafted him in 1985. He had spent five years on one of their farm teams before emerging in the major leagues. Recently, he had ended an eight-year romantic relationship.

Halle later said of the new man in her life: "I knew the minute I saw him face-to-face that I was going to marry him." She further reasoned of her newfound love: "From the beginning we decided to tell each other everything, even if it was painful. I didn't think I'd find somebody who had the same values and was brought up the same way as I was."

The whirlwind romance between the attractive, high-profile couple culminated on New Year's Day 1993, when they married in Atlanta. After their honeymoon in the Caribbean, the couple settled, briefly, into their new house in Georgia. However, with the particular demands of each of their careers, the newlyweds were not destined to spend much time at home together. Although Halle tried to arrange her job offers to mesh with her husband's baseball career, she knew that she could not turn down too many assignments or she would quickly lose her appeal to Hollywood producers. She was well aware that at age 25 she had only so many good years ahead as a leading lady before prime acting roles would be grabbed away by younger talent.

As such, like her equally ambitious husband, Halle tried to balance her career with marriage. However, the couple's home life often took a backseat to the constant pull of fame, fortune, and professional opportunities.

4

BUILDING A HOLLYWOOD NAME

Alex Haley was the Pulitzer Prize–winning author of *Roots,* an elaborate novel based on his ancestors' struggle as slaves in the American South. The book was made into an award-winning television miniseries that had several follow-ups. In 1992 Haley died of a heart attack as he was writing the book *Queen.* (The 1993 book was completed by screenwriter David Stevens.) Haley's new work focused on his real-life great-grandmother who bore a baby girl (Queen) to her white slave master. The book traces the traumatic history of Queen as she experiences a series of hardships due to her mixed-blood background and her lifelong search for self-identity. She eventually finds happiness—albeit briefly—with a ferryboat operator, by whom she gives birth to Simon, who is Haley's father.

CBS-TV contracted to turn Haley's work into a three-part, six-hour miniseries. When Halle learned that the project was now in the casting stage, she set out to win the pivotal role. Although she had no confusion about her racial identity, she strongly identified with the lead part: "I realized that, had I been born a hundred years ago, this could be my story. Queen's life could have been my life. And that was horrifying."

Despite her affinity for the demanding part, Berry had a difficult time being auditioned by the project's director, John Erman. He and the show's producers explained their reasons—all of which were too familiar to Halle from past frustrating casting experiences: "We loved her acting, but we thought she was too beautiful, too young. We thought her skin was too tight, too perfect to make her age to a 72-year-old. And we didn't know how someone so innocent could muster the maturity to play someone so old."

To fight for this demanding major assignment, Halle volunteered to pay for her own airfare, hotel accommodations, and makeup artist to show the producer in a special audition that she could handle all that the character required. Her determination paid dividends and she won the crucial title role—her first lead in a screen project.

Queen was filmed both on Hollywood soundstages and on location in South Carolina. Early in the filming, Halle seriously injured herself when she toppled off a horse and hurt

In the 1993 miniseries Queen, *Halle proved her versatility as an actor by taking on the tough and unglamorous lead role.* (Photofest)

her tailbone. As a result, the costly production was forced to shut down for two weeks while she recouped from the severe accident. Because costar Danny Glover was already committed to another project in the near future, Halle had to return to work sooner than she should have. She had to rely on heavy medication to help her cope with the pain. On some days, she was in such discomfort that she was brought to the set in an ambulance. For the later segments of the story line, Halle relied on special contact lenses, makeup, and costuming to show her character aging into an old woman. She dealt with all of these grueling obstacles because she felt that the production was "a big responsibility to black people and just people in general."

Queen debuted on February 14, 1993, to great enthusiasm. While the critics had mixed feelings about the lengthy TV melodrama, they agreed that Halle had done well in her role. The *New York Post* enthused, "When Queen rages, Berry shines; it's a very forceful and important performance." *USA Today* endorsed her: "*Queen* will be remembered for Berry's electrifying performance." Although Halle was not nominated for an Emmy Award for her impressive performance, she did win recognition for her role in the category of Best Actress in a TV Movie or Miniseries at the 26th Annual National Association for the Advancement of Colored People (NAACP) Image Awards, held in January 1994.

Besides the physical pain she endured in making *Queen*, the lengthy project took an emotional toll on her. "Towards the end I was such a wreck that no one wanted to be around me. . . . I was biting everybody's heads off. I had lived this woman's life from the age of 15 to 65 as she was sexually abused, beaten, treated like dirt. I really felt the injustice." In the end, Halle said, her portrayal was too much and had begun to affect her personally. "If you're a sensitive human being who has emotions and feelings, then it's difficult not to let some of those tears be real." To gain a fresh perspective on life and her career (at one point after *Queen* she thought of abandoning her career to become a civil rights activist), Berry sought therapy to help her understand and "work through all those emotions," she said. "It took me two months to get myself back to reality."

Keeping Busy Professionally

From the unique acting opportunity provided by *Queen*, Halle returned to the casting battlefields of predominantly white, male-oriented Hollywood. She had a cameo as herself in the weak *CB4* (1993), a rap "mockumentary" starring comedian Chris Rock. Next, she had the unrewarding role of a reporter (originally conceived as a role for a white actor) in the family release *Father Hood* (1993). Roger Ebert of the *Chicago Sun-Times* sympathized with

Berry being stuck in such a bad part: "Her role is not only the most thankless one in this movie, but the most thankless role in any film I have seen this year."

Also in 1993, Berry again had the second lead, this time in a film called *The Program* (1993). Here she is seen as an aristocratic, affluent young woman who tutors an educationally challenged jock (Omar Epps) at a southern college. Halle liked this assignment because it enabled her to play a role so different from her own upbringing. It helped her to avoid the career trap of so many other black talents who could not seem to get beyond clichéd big-screen urban dramas. (This was one reason why Halle rejected a role in 1993's gritty *Menace II Society*.) As Berry expressed her career choices: "I'm so lucky that I'm able to work in this industry, so I don't take it lightly. Black youth today desperately need positive images and role models. So I won't do certain movies."

A Visit to Bedrock

The Flintstones was a hugely successful 1960s TV series, a cartoon show set in the Stone Age that parodied contemporary suburban life. In the early 1990s Universal Pictures and executive producer Steven Spielberg decided to convert the idea into a $45 million live-action movie comedy. John Goodman and Elizabeth Perkins were cast as Fred and Wilma Flintstone with Rick Moranis and Rosie

O'Donnell as their good friends Barney and Betty Rubble. The filmmakers originally thought of actor Sharon Stone for the role of the blond beauty named (coincidentally) Sharon Stone. However, Stone was not interested in this supporting part.

In contrast, Halle was enthusiastic about this role. "I was the symbol of black beauty [in the picture]. Me, a black woman." She also pointed out, "The fact that they

Halle in The Flintstones (Photofest)

cast me says a lot for where we're going in motion pictures today." What especially pleased Berry about the new role was that, unusually, she was playing a part not specifically written for a black woman. Despite the paper-thin characters and flimsy story line of *The Flintstones,* the film did very well at the box office.

Another Gritty Drama

It had been nearly five years since Halle portrayed a street prostitute in Spike Lee's *Jungle Fever.* Now with several demanding acting assignments on her resume she felt well qualified to try such a character again, this time in the feature film *Losing Isaiah* (1995). Halle wanted the part of Khaila Richards, a crack addict living on the rough turf of Chicago's South Side. Khaila deposits her infant in an alleyway garbage container and goes off in search of her next drug fix. When she returns, she finds the container empty. Later, the found baby comes to the attention of a white social worker, who falls in love with the abandoned child and soon adopts him into her family. Three years later, Khaila, now drug-free and with a job, turns up to reclaim her offspring, which leads to a lengthy courtroom confrontation between the two impassioned women.

Once again, beautiful Halle met with skepticism—this time from director Stephen Gyllenhaal—when she

Halle and Marc John Jeffries in Losing Isaiah (Photofest)

requested an audition for the part of Khaila. After much persuasion by Halle and her agent, Gyllenhaal finally agreed to have her read for the role—largely as a courtesy. Rising to the challenge and overlooking the seeming slight to her past acting credits, Berry went through the paces of a highly dramatic sequence for 51 takes. Once again she proved herself artistically viable and gained the prized role.

Berry related well to her costar Jessica Lange, another former model who had spent years overcoming her stereotype as "merely" a beautiful mannequin, and who had gone on to win two Academy Awards.

The R-rated *Losing Isaiah* debuted in March 1995 to disappointing critical response. Rita Kempley of the *Washington Post* complained that the film contained "only a few moments that expose the human beings beneath the P.C. [politically correct] symbols." Made for $17 million, *Losing Isaiah* only grossed $8.5 million in worldwide distribution. Halle was nominated for, but did not win, an NAACP Image Award as Outstanding Actress in a Motion Picture for her role in the film.

After portraying a street character, Halle made a startling change of pace when she accepted the colead in the Showtime cable TV production of *Solomon & Sheba*. Cast as Nikhaule, who becomes the queen of Sheba, she shared the spotlight with Jimmy Smits (a colead of the TV series

NYPD Blue), who played the king of Israel. When Berry was asked why she had accepted this role, she reasoned, "Anytime it's something where a black woman wouldn't be the obvious choice, I really go after it." Halle's rationale was based on the fact that, in the past, Hollywood had utilized white performers to play the Ethiopian monarch. Premiering on American TV in late February 1995, *Solomon & Sheba* was no masterpiece, but it provided obvious entertainment for most viewers. For her efforts, Halle was nominated for another NAACP Image Award as Outstanding Actress in a Television Movie, Miniseries, but again lost the prize.

Box-Office Duty

The year 1996 proved to be one of Halle's busiest on screen. Her friend and mentor, producer Joel Silver, hired Halle for *Executive Decision*, a big-budget thriller. She was cast as a gutsy flight attendant aboard an airplane that has been skyjacked by terrorists. Kurt Russell (as a civilian scientist) and Steven Seagal (as a military expert) are the heroes who board the jet plane in midair to combat the villains, with Halle's character providing brave support. The long action film was a moderate crowd pleaser.

When questioned why she chose the relatively undemanding *Executive Decision* role, Halle noted that her $1 million salary was a definite deciding factor. (She used

Halle took on a leading role in a big-budget thriller in Executive Decision. (Photofest)

part of her healthy fee to buy her mother an impressive two-story home in a Cleveland suburb.) In contrast, she accepted top billing in *Race the Sun* (1996) because it allowed her to portray an exemplary, true-life character. She was Miss Sandra Beecher, a spunky new teacher at Kona Pali High School on the big island of Hawaii. Although Beecher's classroom specialty is English, she is assigned to teach a science class. There she instills self-worth into her students (a group of self-professed losers) by guiding them in the building of a prizewinning solar-powered vehicle.

The PG-rated *Race the Sun* won little favor with the critics, who thought it took too much from older, better feel-good feature films. Halle received mixed lackluster reviews for her lead role in this film.

Next came a cameo as herself in Spike Lee's *Girl 6* (1996), followed by *The Rich Man's Wife* (1996), in which Halle won the title role. (When she first received the script she wondered, "They've offered it to me—what's

Christopher McDonald and Halle in the murder mystery The Rich Man's Wife *(Photofest)*

wrong with it?") Halle liked this assignment because the role was a change of pace for her. She said, "This movie allowed me to do something different from other roles I've played. It's a murder mystery, *film noir* kind of movie, which I've wanted to do for a long time." Halle was modest about performing the title part. "I'd be lying if I said that I didn't feel pressure, but I also know why I'm doing what I'm doing, and I'm really doing this because I love to act."

Working on *The Rich Man's Wife* also gave Halle her first opportunity to work with a female film director, Amy Holden Jones. Jones had scripted *Mystic Pizza* (1988) and *Indecent Proposal* (1993), for which Halle had auditioned, but lost out to Demi Moore. The plot revolves around an unhappily married woman (Berry) who confides to a bizarre stranger her great unhappiness with her wealthy, despicable spouse. The stranger, a deranged soul, follows out her fantasy wish and kills the husband, leaving Halle's character as a prime suspect in the homicide. *The Rich Man's Wife* proved to be both an artistic and commercial flop. At least publicly, Halle gave no apology for the unsatisfying film. Not only had it allowed her to work with one of Hollywood's relatively few women directors, but "I got to be colorless for three months and feel what white leading ladies feel every time out."

With so many film assignments to her credit, Halle Berry should have been a contented woman. However, her personal life had fallen to a new low and, in 1996, her marriage to baseball's David Justice was coming to an end.

5

A TRAUMATIC NEW BEGINNING

In the midst of Halle Berry's nonstop filmmaking activity during 1995–96 she said, "I love to be in front of the camera. It's what I get the most pleasure from."

The truth of this statement became evident when her marriage to David Justice ended in 1996. Even back in 1993, a few months after the couple's whirlwind courtship and hasty marriage, the seemingly lighthearted Halle was already mentioning the many differences between she and her groom. He loved sports; she could not care less about them, although she tried to appreciate baseball for his sake. She was neat at home, while he was messy. She also observed, "When I'm trying to sleep, he's in bed watching *Sports Center*. I have to get up early, and he sleeps until midday."

From the start, the demands of their professions kept the high-profile, handsome couple apart, usually on opposite coasts. Whenever they were together, they found it increasingly difficult to discuss topics of mutual interest. Furthermore, Halle did not care for life in Georgia, where David was so well known, and David felt anonymous and out of place in Hollywood, where Halle worked and where the couple had a second home.

Given the mounting troubles in her marriage, Halle made it clear that she could not abandon acting—even temporarily. Looking back on this pivotal career versus personal life choice, she stated, "I started doing movies again. That created more separation. Our relationship started to fizzle. I became a madwoman trying to save it. Blaming myself a lot—if I'd never left, if I were a better wife . . . I know now had I never left I would have died. Faded away." Unknown to the public at the time, during this trying period Halle had grown extremely depressed and had even fantasized about committing suicide. As she had in the past, she sought psychological counseling to deal with her problems.

As part of regaining a healthy emotional perspective, Halle underwent a great deal of self-examination. In the process she discovered, "I was living a superficial existence," and that she must "really take ownership for that." Part of her realization included, "When you're a so-called celebrity, it's very easy not to deal with yourself because everybody is loving you, everybody is giving you things, everybody is doing so much for you that you don't have to do anything for yourself."

Another result of her self-examination was to realize "there was a deep spiritual being inside me, but I was afraid to let that be seen for fear of rejection, fear of judgment, fear of not being this person the public had made me out to be." Trying to live up to her self-imposed celebrity image led Halle to be in public denial of her problems for a long time, especially regarding her faltering marriage.

The End of the Marriage

The low point of the couple's marriage occurred on February 18, 1996. Justice was to report that day for spring training with the Atlanta Braves in West Palm Beach, Florida. However, earlier that Sunday he was detained by the police in nearby Riviera Beach. Allegedly he had been spotted in a run-down part of town that was long associated with drug deals and prostitution. When law enforcers approached Justice's car, they witnessed a man fleeing from the scene. Reportedly the deputies discovered a stack of money fanned out on the passenger side of the vehicle. Justice was sitting behind the wheel. While he was temporarily detained by the officers, he was not

Halle and former husband David Justice in 1993 (Associated Press)

arrested, as they found no drugs in the car or on the sports star. The incident received heavy media coverage.

While Justice continued to proclaim his innocence and denied that he had ever cheated on Berry, within a month of that episode, Halle (in California) and David (in Georgia) filed for divorce. It was revealed later that the couple had realized their marriage was beyond repair by their third wedding anniversary. Halle had been as stubborn about her marriage as she had always been about her career; she had wanted the couple to seek marital counseling, but Justice was already prepared to admit defeat. As a result, Halle experienced a perplexing mixture of emotions, including denial and anger. This, in turn, led to bitter divorce proceedings.

As Halle experienced great frustration over the divorce, she also became determined to make telephone contact with her long-absent father. "I got him on the phone and unleashed all this anger. I released it. I told him how much he had hurt me by abandoning our family, by not being in my life when I was a child. At the end of the conversation, I think he said, 'I'm sorry.'" That and two other highly charged phone calls were the last direct communications that the star had with her father before his death.

Halle attempted to remove all evidence of David Justice from her life, including a tattoo she had bearing her husband's name. But still she could not eradicate the defeat of the failed marriage. As she told *Ebony* magazine in 1997, "I took my dogs, and I went in the garage and sat in the car. For two or three hours, I just cried and I cried. . . . I think that's the weakest I have ever been in my life. That's what the breakup of my marriage did to me. It took away my self-esteem." Halle later admitted that she had contemplated suicide during this period. As she confided to TV interviewer Barbara Walters in 2002, "Something was telling [me] on the right side my brain, 'Girl, don't do it! Girl, don't do it! Think of your mother.' . . . I couldn't do that to her."

When Vince Cirrincione, her longtime manager, learned of Halle's emotional plight he contacted Halle's mother and urged her to come out to Los Angeles to be with her distraught daughter. Thanks to her family and friends, Halle got past this bleak period. Eventually she and David Justice reached a civil divorce settlement. In retrospect, she realized of this traumatic stage in her life, "I think I was still using men and my mate to identify who I was. And when that was gone, I was nothing."

Revlon to the Rescue

In the midst of Halle's divorce, she received special and much-needed validation from Revlon Cosmetics, which hired her to be the new spokesperson for their world-famous firm. Berry accepted the lucrative, prestigious assignment after careful consideration. In the past she had rejected offers that would have made her the endorser of beauty projects just for black women. She wanted, as with her film roles, to be a nonethnic representative for any merchandise she promoted. But Revlon wished her to be its spokesperson across the board, which indicated that black women were included in the company's major products. "We don't need a special line just for us," Halle said. "That's making us too different."

Halle had concerns that the high-profile Revlon job might only reinforce her status as a former model and beauty queen, that it might overshadow her abilities as an established performer. Eventually she decided that her acting credentials spoke for themselves, and she took the very lucrative Revlon deal.

Laughing for Pay

Halle knew that she needed a change of pace in her acting career to help her out of her low emotional state after her divorce. Thus, she accepted the lead in

Although the film B*A*P*S *was a box-office failure, critics admired Halle's ability to shine in the lightest of roles. She is pictured here on the right with costar Natalie Desselle.* (Photofest)

B*A*P*S (1997), a screwball comedy directed by Robert Townsend, a veteran black filmmaker. Said Halle of the unsophisticated farce, "Probably it's the best medicine I could ask for."

Halle was cast as Nisi, a fashion-challenged Georgia waitress who, along with a hairdresser friend, has a dream of one day opening a combination restaurant–beauty salon. The only problem is that these two clueless souls are without any funds for their enterprise. The zany duo embarks on a trip to Los Angeles to raise the money, with unanticipated results.

Critical reviews of *B*A*P*S* were generally poor. Janet Maslin of the *New York Times* had little use for this "bad, amateur, poor and silly" movie. However, she noted of Halle's presence in this comedy, "Even with gold teeth, prehensile fingernails, whipped-cream blond hair and a squeeze-tight orange plastic jumpsuit, she's still absolutely beautiful."

Oprah Winfrey and Warren Beatty Help Out

Among Halle's most enduring role models is Oprah Winfrey. Berry admired how this African American woman had become a self-made phenomenon as a TV talk show host, movie notable, film and TV producer, and philanthropist. Berry was flattered when Winfrey asked her to star in *The Wedding*, a TV movie to be produced by

Oprah's Harpo Productions. Based on Dorothy West's 1995 novel, the multigenerational story was set largely in the early 1950s in New England. Halle's character Shelby Coles, a black woman from an elite, well-established family, is about to wed a struggling white jazz musician (played by Eric Thal). Before the sumptuous wedding takes place, the heroine encounters a black man (Carl Lumbly) who tries to convince her to marry him instead. The highly publicized film did adequately in the ratings and earned Halle positive critical response. Matt Roush (*USA Today*) offered, "Halle Berry is simply radiant as . . . the pampered princess of an affluent mixed-race family." Halle was again nominated for an NAACP Image Award for this performance.

From the small-screen film *The Wedding*, Halle jumped into big-screen fare with 1998's *Bulworth*. Her leading man was 1960s heartthrob Warren Beatty, who not only wrote the story and screenplay (in collaboration), but also produced and directed the film. Beatty plays a veteran California senator who is tired of his shady past and sees no future for himself. Thus, the politician decides to freely speak his mind in public, which causes a stir in the political arena. In the process, he meets a gorgeous fledgling black rap artist (played by Halle). The unlikely duo soon falls in love. To his amazement, he discovers that his beloved is a contract killer he had hired.

Halle and Warren Beatty in Bulworth (Photofest)

Responding to why she had accepted Beatty's request to join him in *Bulworth,* Halle said, "I just love doing different things, and that's the challenge of it. This was a lot of fun for me, another different character." While *Bulworth* received mixed critical reviews and did only average business at the box office, Berry was pleased to add this satirical feature to her acting resume. She also was proud that after filming ended she could count Beatty as a new friend and mentor, a person always ready to advise her on upcoming career moves. For *Bulworth,* Halle received yet another NAACP Image Award nomination.

Rounding out 1998, Halle costarred in *Why Do Fools Fall in Love?*, a story about three women who are battling one another over the estate of a deceased musician. Halle plays a Los Angeles–based R&B singer, the glamorous woman who, for a time, was the love of the musician's troubled life. Directed by Gregory Nava, *Why Do Fools Fall in Love?* lacked sufficient freshness and vitality to make a strong impression on moviegoers.

Fortunately for Halle, after this relative film misfire, her next screen project—1999's *Introducing Dorothy Dandridge*—would provide both a major challenge and a great success in her career. It was the role that she felt she had been born to play.

6

INSPIRED BY DOROTHY DANDRIDGE

Growing up, Halle Berry had often seen and enjoyed the 1954 film *Carmen Jones* on TV. As a result, she became fascinated with Dorothy Dandridge (1922–65), the stunning, vibrant black performer who played the lead role in this all-black screen musical. Berry said later, "I knew I wanted to be an actress just because of her and how she jumped off the screen."

As time passed, Berry was further impressed to learn that Dandridge had received a Best Actress Academy Award nomination for her *Carmen Jones* performance. (Dandridge was the first African American talent to receive such an Oscar honor in the entire history of the awards show, but she lost the prize to Grace Kelly of *The Country Girl*.) What really intrigued Halle was discovering

Dorothy Dandrige was a major inspiration for Halle's acting career. (Landov)

that both she and Dorothy had been born in the same Cleveland hospital, albeit many years apart.

As time went on, Halle kept adding to her knowledge of the iconic Dandridge, an ill-fated artist whose show business career was severely restricted by racial prejudice. The daughter of budding performer Ruby Dandridge (who had developed her own show business career), Dorothy and her older sister Vivian grew up in a single-parent home (their minister father had left the household months before Dorothy was born). As children, Dorothy and Vivian toured the South, performing at churches and social functions. By the late 1930s the teenage sisters obtained bits in major studio movies in Hollywood.

By the early 1940s Dorothy was married to Harold Nicholas, who was half of a famous dancing brothers act. She and Harold had a daughter born with brain damage, which not only helped to ruin their marriage, but also made Dandridge permanently guilt-ridden about her child's handicap. Meanwhile, largely due to racial prejudice in Hollywood (reflecting the attitudes of the time in America), Dorothy found worthy screen parts almost impossible to come by. Rejected in the film medium, she turned to nightclub engagements across the United States. Like Lena Horne, another African American performer who could not get a proper break in the movie industry of the 1940s and 1950s, Dandridge made her show business reputation as a sultry vocalist in expensive venues.

Always anxious to somehow make a success in movies despite the great odds against her, Dorothy later accepted the demeaning role of a jungle queen in *Tarzan's Peril* (1951). Things improved for her somewhat with *Bright Road* (1953). Next came her striking success in *Carmen Jones* (1954). Thereafter, however, Dandridge found her dream of building a real mainstream movie career dashed by the lack of decent acting options available. It led to Dorothy performing in such unworthy films as *The Decks Ran Red* (1958). Dandridge's final big-league movie assignment was joining Sidney Poitier for the musical *Porgy and Bess* (1959).

Thereafter, the disillusioned Dandridge returned to singing in clubs. Throughout the coming years she kept hoping for a movie comeback, but that dream was never fulfilled. This was due to a mixture of racial prejudice, Dorothy's growing drinking problem, bad career management, and the effects of the passing years. During an emotional ebb, Dandridge ended her life in September 1965. She was only 41 years old at the time. When she died, she was nearly broke despite having earned $1 million during her decades-long entertainment career.

Making the Dream Come True

In 1991 Earl Mills, Dandridge's longtime manager, wrote the biography *Dorothy Dandridge: A Portrait in Black*. Halle, who had maintained her strong interest in Dandridge's inspirational and troubled life, asked her own manager, Vincent Cirrincione, to acquire the screen rights to the book so that Berry could star in a screen adaptation of the star's life. To Berry's dismay, she learned that another party had already optioned the title. Then, in 1997, Donald Bogle's definitive biography of Dandridge was published. Again, before Halle could step in to acquire the screen rights, the property was optioned by film and song star Whitney Houston.

Despite the stiff competition and the many obstacles, Halle persisted in her belief that somehow one day, she would star on camera in the Dorothy Dandridge story. When Berry learned that the current option on Mills's book had expired, she jumped in and gained control of the screen rights to this biography.

However, the seven-year struggle to bring the Dorothy Dandridge story to the screen was still not over. As executive producer of the project, Halle had to find mainstream financial backing for the film. When no movie studio expressed serious interest in the project, Halle thought about making the film on a smaller scale—perhaps as an

$8 or $10 million TV movie. Finally, the HBO cable network agreed to package and air the production.

Martha Coolidge was selected to direct the mature account of the sensitive, tormented Dandridge, with Halle playing the lead role. (Performer Wendie Williams provided the dubbed-in singing voice of Dandridge.)

Just as she was driven to get this cherished project onto the drawing board, Halle was equally determined

Halle and Klaus Maria Brandauer in Introducing Dorothy Dandridge. *Working on this film was one of the high points in Halle's life.* (Photofest)

to do justice to the tortured life of this pioneer in the integration of the American film business. Halle's empathy for her role model was enormous, especially because she saw great similarities in both their lives of striving against great odds for professional success and personal happiness. During the tightly scheduled shoot, several scenes suddenly had to be deleted to keep the film within its budget. Berry came to the rescue by donating part of her salary to finance some of the needed sequences.

In the process of starring in *Introducing Dorothy Dandridge,* Halle had revelations about her own life: "I realized I had to stop blaming my father for all the things that were wrong in my relationships. While his absence was part of it, a lot had to do with me and my choices. I would say I wanted somebody real in my life, but then I would be attracted to the superficial."

After a special August 14, 1999, premiere in Halle and Dandridge's hometown of Cleveland, *Introducing Dorothy Dandridge* debuted on HBO the next week. The reviews were full of praise. The trade paper *Daily Variety* judged, "As Dandridge, Berry is sexy and innocent, breathy and every bit as beautiful as the glamorous star. The role is that of a damaged beauty—but not a pitiful one—and Berry hits the mark whether it calls for sultry or sullen." *Newsweek* magazine agreed, labeling Halle's acting "an evocation of the beauty and electricity that made Dandridge a legend."

As a reward for bringing *Introducing Dorothy Dandridge* to the screen—and for her sterling performance—Halle garnered a host of industry awards: a Golden Globe, Screen Actors Guild Award, an Emmy Award for Outstanding Actress in a Miniseries or Movie, as well as an NAACP Image Award in the same category. (She also won a 1999 Image Award as Entertainer of the Year.)

The success of *Introducing Dorothy Dandridge* remains a high point in Halle's life.

A New Romantic Interest

When Halle was making her acceptance speech at the Golden Globe Awards on January 23, 2000, she acknowledged a new man in her life, singer Eric Benét. She told him in front of the TV cameras, "You have given me the biggest gift anybody can give me, and that is the freedom to be who I am and for loving me anyway."

According to Halle, she initially met Benét a few years earlier through a mutual friend and then got to know him through several e-mail chats. In his account of their dating history, he remembers, "We used to go to the same L.A. mall. And she'd often come up and say hi. From there, we just began hanging out, and before you know it, we were an item."

Eric Benét Jordan was born in Milwaukee, Wisconsin, in 1967, one of four children in a middle-class household. His father was a policeman and his mother, a homemaker, had a love of singing. The laid-back Eric grew to be a handsome teenager whose looks made him popular with young women. He was in a vocal group with his sister and cousin, and they eventually signed a deal with Capitol Records.

Singer Eric Benét and Halle Berry (Landov)

Eric soon became a solo act and signed with Warner Bros. Records. His first disc for his new label was *True to Myself* (1996), which included the R&B number "Spend My Life With You," a chart-topping hit that was nominated for a Grammy award.

While Eric's career was on an upward track, he suffered several personal losses. His father died of cancer in the early 1990s. In 1992 his former partner, Tami Stauff, died as a result of a car crash, leaving him to raise India, the couple's 13-month-old daughter. For a time, the depressed man abandoned singing to work for the UPS delivery service. When his spirits revived, he returned to singing, performing both on tour and in the recording studio.

Not only was Halle attracted by the handsome, sensitive, creative Benét, but she was also drawn to his seven-year-old daughter, India. Having longed for children of her own, Berry happily took on the role of substitute mother.

A Driving Disaster

With the success of *Introducing Dorothy Dandridge* and the growing importance of Eric Benét in her personal life, Halle felt that she had all the essential bases covered. She had accepted a costarring role in *X-Men* (2000), a big-budget sci-fi thriller based on a highly successful comic book. After several months of filming the project in Canada she was back in Los Angeles.

Early on the morning of Wednesday, February 23, 2000, Halle was returning to her Hollywood Hills home after spending an evening with a friend. As her rented car reached an intersection, she had a recollection of "vaguely seeing something dark" to her right. After that, she claimed that everything was a blank. Her next memory was of reaching her own home and that, soon thereafter, her boyfriend Eric Benét was at her side. Benét noticed the serious gash on Berry's forehead and that she was bleeding profusely. He immediately drove her to the hospital emergency room. There she received more than 20 stitches to close the gash. (Later Halle would undergo plastic surgery to remove any scar traces.)

At the same time Halle was receiving medical attention at Cedars-Sinai, 27-year-old Heta Raythata, a Santa Monica, California-based accountant and realtor, was at the same hospital receiving emergency treatment for a broken wrist. Despite the pain and trauma of Heta's injury, she was excited to spot a movie notable, Halle, receiving medical care at a nearby hospital workstation.

As was later revealed in an official report, Berry had driven her car through a red light on Sunset Boulevard and collided with the 1996 Pontiac Sunfire driven by Raythata. The impact set Heta's car on fire and, for a time, the victim was trapped inside. According to an eyewitness at the scene, Halle had reportedly driven away, leaving Raythata endangered. The witness had phoned for an ambulance, which rescued Heta and then transported her to Cedars-Sinai for medical treatment.

At the hospital, the dazed Berry informed an off-duty police officer of the few facts she could remember of the accident. The next morning she filed a formal report with the West Hollywood's Sheriff Department. Thereafter the police impounded Halle's car, which was rented, but did not arrest the terrified celebrity. Eventually, the district attorney charged Halle only with a misdemeanor count, not a criminal charge.

Upon recovering from her trauma, Raythata was upset that no criminal charges had been filed against Halle for having seemingly caused an accident and then leaving the scene without apparent concern for the victim. Halle insisted to the police—and to the media—that her only explanation for the strange sequence of events was that she must have blacked out before reviving at home and then being taken for medical assistance.

During the weeks following the car accident, Halle did not sit idly by. As she told *In Style* magazine in July 2000: "I've spent two months basically talking to doctors and experts. Football players get banged in the head and then go on to play a whole game because it's *overlearned* behavior. Driving the two blocks to my house, that's overlearned behavior for me." Although comforted by what medical specialists told her, Halle was badly shaken by her bizarre behavior at the accident scene. She noted to the press, "I had lost track of 20 minutes. I had also lost track of my self-esteem."

Raythata filed a civil suit against Berry, claiming that the accident had left Raythata with permanent disability. That suit was settled out of court for an undisclosed amount, but the unpleasant episode tainted Halle's once-sterling image.

Three days after the high-profile civil suit was resolved, Halle pleaded no contest to the misdemeanor charge (meaning that she accepted responsibility for the charge without an official admission of guilt). She was fined $13,500, put on three years' probation regarding driving, and was required to perform 200 hours of community service. In her courtroom response Halle told the judge, "I am pleased that this can be resolved." She also commented, "Community service is part of what I do anyway. Resolving it this way allows me to take some responsibility." She concluded with, "Now I can look at myself in the mirror. Thank God no one was killed. There were blessings that night."

X-Men to the Rescue

After the nightmare of the car accident and its aftermath, which could have permanently sidetracked her show business career, Halle was glad to be the subject of professional and not personal publicity with the release of *X-Men* in mid-2000. Made on a hefty $75 million budget and directed by Bryan Singer, *X-Men* was based on the popular Marvel Comics property. It concerned a group of genetic mutants with special powers, led by wheelchair-bound Charles Xavier, a telepath. Known as Professor X, he trains

Halle played the mutant Storm in the successful action film X-Men *and its sequel,* X-Men 2. (Photofest)

and organizes mutants into using their special powers to combat evil.

Berry joined the cast of *X-Men* in the role of Storm, a mutant who uses high-powered winds and lighting to combat dastardly opponents. The part called for Halle to wear an array of formfitting black-leather outfits, and she was saddled with a bizarrely styled platinum-colored wig, and, through special effects, boasted unflattering opaque white orbs for eyes.

When *X-Men* reached the multiplexes in July 2000 it proved enormously popular with young moviegoers, even if most reviewers were less than ecstatic about the predictable good-versus-evil narrative. *X-Men* grossed

$157.2 million in domestic release and piled up a total of $300 million in worldwide distribution. With such a success, a sequel was immediately put into the works, with key participants—including Halle—contracted to return for the next film.

7

CLAIMING HER OSCAR

At the August 1999 Cleveland premiere of *Introducing Dorothy Dandridge*, Eric Benét proposed marriage to Halle Berry. Although the couple had been together for more than two years, Halle was still smarting from her failed marriage with David Justice. As such, she was in no hurry to remarry. Finally, at the start of 2001 with the ordeal of Berry's car mishap finally behind her, the duo set a marriage date. On that January 24, the couple were legally united at a quiet southern California beach with a few friends and relatives attending. It was not until early the next month that the famous newlyweds made their marriage known to the public.

Back in Front of the Cameras

Having enjoyed making *X-Men*, Halle next contracted to make another action flick, *Swordfish* (2001), this time choosing to work again for her longtime friend, producer Joel Silver. She was reunited with her *X-Men* costar Hugh Jackman in this thriller starring John Travolta. The high-tech, expensive special-effects film focuses on a world-class spy (played by Travolta) who, with the help of a talented computer hacker (Jackman), attempts to steal $9.5 billion in government funds. Halle plays Ginger, the attractive woman who assists the two in their cyber-space scheme.

In *Swordfish,* for which she was paid a $2.5 million salary, Halle agreed to appear partially nude in a scene.

Halle and John Travolta in the action film Swordfish (Photofest)

Rationalizing her artistic decision—after years of refus-
ing to do on-screen nudity—Berry confided to *Essence*
magazine, "My husband, Eric, was actually the one who
told me to stop worrying about pleasing others and to
start pleasing myself. . . . My refusal [in the past to do on-
screen nudity] was strange, because I've been comfortable with my sexuality for a long time. Throughout my
home I have sculptures and paintings celebrating the
naked body, which I feel represents freedom and grace."
She further explained that she had previously felt inhib-
ited because of her responsibilities as a top African
American actor: "I felt myself carrying the hopes and
dreams of my community on my back." But after careful
consideration of how the scene would affect her career
and reputation, Halle agreed to the seminude scene.
Although the film was a box-office disappointment, Halle
won an NAACP Image Award as Outstanding Actress in
a Motion Picture.

A Work of Substance

Among the many screenplays being tossed around Hollywood at this time was *Monster's Ball*. Back in 1995 Robert
De Niro and Marlon Brando were scheduled to costar in
the movie drama with actor Sean Penn as director. Those
plans fell through, as did later hopes for Oliver Stone to
direct the project with Tommy Lee Jones as a star. A few

Halle in her award-winning role as Leticia with costar Billy Bob Thornton in Monster's Ball *(Photofest)*

years passed, and *Monster's Ball* was still making the rounds of Hollywood producers, without finding financing or star names attached.

Eventually the film property came to Halle's attention. Even before she finished reading the script she was excited by the project. Once again Berry had to combat her image as a glamorous movie star to be considered for the role of the drab waitress in an outlying area of Georgia. In the film, Halle plays the downtrodden Leticia Musgrove, whose imprisoned husband is on death row. Everything seems against her. Shortly after her husband's execution, her son is killed in a vehicular accident. She is in danger of losing her job as a waitress, her house is about to be foreclosed, and her old car is falling apart.

Leticia encounters a prison guard—a white racist—not knowing that he was the one who executed her husband. He, too, is an unhappy soul, grieving for the loss of his son, also a prison guard, who has recently killed himself. As time progresses, the two troubled individuals find comfort with one another.

When Halle requested to audition for *Monster's Ball*, producer Lee Daniels was initially against considering her for the key part: "She's so beautiful. I couldn't see her as this beaten-down woman at the end of her rope." But eventually both Daniels and director Marc Foster changed their opinion. Said Foster, "I thought she'd be too [glamorous], but I saw she'd be willing to deglamorize herself. I also saw incredible sadness in her eyes from her past. I thought I'd be able to tap into that." After much persuasion, Halle was eventually hired for the part at a bargain price of $100,000. She joined a cast that included Billy Bob Thornton (as Hank Grotowski, the racist prison guard), Peter Boyle (as Hank's bigoted old father), Heath Ledger (as Sonny, Hank's son), and Sean "P. Diddy" Combs (as Leticia's doomed mate).

Monster's Ball opened in late 2001 to qualify for the upcoming Oscar sweepstakes. The film impressed most critics. Peter Travers (*Rolling Stone*) labeled it a "rubbed raw" drama and observed of Halle's emotional performance: "Berry—playing against type in the performance to beat among actresses this year—is volcanic." Stephen Hunter (*Washington Post*) found the grim tale uplifting and reported of Halle: "She has deglamorized herself to an amazing degree and taken up a compellingly believable rural accent." Roger Ebert (*Chicago Sun-Times*) said, "Billy Bob Thornton and Halle Berry star as Hank and Leticia, in two performances that are so powerful because they observe the specific natures of these two characters, and avoid the pitfalls of racial clichés."

With excellent word of mouth, *Monster's Ball* did very well at the box office. The powerful film was well represented when it came time for industry awards. In particular, Halle won a Best Actress Prize at the Screen Guild Awards, the Berlin International Film Festival, the Chicago Film Critics Association Awards, the Black Reel Awards, the National Board of Review, and, most impressively, at the 74th Annual Academy Awards in March 2002.

Rarely has any performer exhibited such high emotion as when Halle walked to the podium to accept her Best Actress Oscar from the prior year's Best Actor, Russell

Crowe. An overwhelmed Berry could not stop crying with joy. As her husband Eric Benét observed, "It looked like she was about to completely lose it [and faint]." In her highly charged acceptance speech, among the many individuals she thanked was director Marc Foster: "This moviemaking experience was magical for me because of you. You believed in me, you trusted me, and you gently guided me to very scary places."

Later, when Halle met with the international media backstage, the still overwhelmed Berry voiced her thoughts regarding her Oscar victory and what it meant to the further integration of American show business. "I never thought this would be possible in my lifetime. I hope we will start to be judged on our merits and our works. This moment, it's not really just about me. It's about so many people that went before me. It's about people who are fighting alongside me and now it will be indelibly easier."

Another Broken Trust

Unfortunately, Halle hardly had time to enjoy the career high of her Oscar win. Tabloids were reporting that her husband, Eric Benét, was engaged in a longtime affair with another woman. While Benét and Berry denied the supermarket newspapers' revelations, the mainstream press began to report that the couple's marriage was in serious difficulty. Halle reportedly had decided to remain supportive of Eric, saying, "Marriage is about sticking together through the tough times." She also took this stance because she had adopted his young daughter, India, and did not want to disrupt the child's life. (Said Berry of her special bond with the youngster, "I used to come home for solitude and quiet. Now I come home for love.")

Although the celebrity couple put on a good face whenever they were seen in public together—which was far less frequently than they had been before—as the months passed the marriage bonds further disintegrated. In October 2003, having attempted marital counseling and other remedies, the duo separated officially. A philo- sophical Berry told the press of her domestic breakup, "I'm getting used to it. I've made some bad choices in that area. I used to say that if there was a loser in town, I'd find him. But I don't say that anymore. I'm going to find the right man." In April 2004 Berry filed for divorce from Benét.

Getting on with Her Career

While Halle's home life was in turmoil throughout much of 2002, she turned her attention back to her career. Before she won her Oscar for *Monster's Ball*, she had accepted a decorative role as Jinx, one of super agent James Bond's love interests in the 007 screen exploit *Die*

Another Day (2002). In this action film, Halle was cast as a slinky undercover agent for America's National Security Agency. When asked why a performer of her stature would take such a picture assignment, Berry said, "You have to balance the art with the commercial projects because it's very much about the business part of it today." During the athletic four-month shoot, Berry was injured on the set by a smoke-grenade detonation. It left a sliver of the casing lodged in her left eye. Emergency surgery repaired the damage, but Berry had a swollen, sore eye for some time thereafter.

Halle plays a criminal psychologist in the horror film Gothika. (Photofest)

Next, Berry repeated her role of Storm in *X-2: X-Men United* (2003), the much-anticipated sequel to *X-Men*. A few months later Halle starred in *Gothika*, a horror thriller (produced by Joel Silver) that featured Robert Downey Jr., Penelope Cruz, and Charles S. Dutton. In this suspense tale she was cast as Miranda Grey, a criminal psychologist. During the Canadian shoot, the accident-prone Berry suffered an on-set mishap and broke her arm. The film's production schedule had to be reworked because of Halle's injury. Although *Gothika* was roasted by most critics, it did reasonably well in theaters.

The Hardworking Oscar Winner

Unable (or unwilling) to slow down her professional pace in the new millennium, Halle has continued to lend her box-office clout to upcoming film projects. In *Catwoman* (2004), based on the DC Comics character, Halle plays Patience Prince, whose alter ego is the title figure of the film. Employing her special powers for a mixture of seeming good and evil purposes, she is trailed by a detective (played by Benjamin Bratt) and finds that another highly capable woman (portrayed by Sharon Stone) is her chief adversary. Also upcoming for Berry is *The Set-Up*, a remake of a well-regarded 1940s film about corruption in boxing.

Halle is scheduled to be producer and star of *Nappily Ever After*, a "serious comedy" directed by Patricia Car-

Halle shows no sign of slowing down her career. (Landov)

dosa. In *The Guide*, Halle will reteam with her *Die Another Day* director, Lee Tamahori. In this action thriller she portrays a Native American of the Seneca tribe who has the gift of helping desperate people escape bad situations by erasing their pasts and providing them with fresh identities. Halle will be lending her voice to the animated sci-fi film *Robots* (2005), in which she will play Cappy, a sexy corporate robot who seduces an idealistic young genius who is trying to improve the world through his inventions.

Looking to the Future

As Halle Berry, named Favorite Actress at the June 2004 BET Awards, continues to pursue her acting craft, she retains an unwavering faith in her ability to challenge the slowly changing racial and gender bias in Hollywood. Her motto continues to be, "I don't like taking no. I fight for roles. I want the same shot as everyone else." Reflecting on her successful rise to fame and fortune despite many adversities, the Oscar winner says, "When you go through bad times, you find where your great capacity to learn is. And I've been through really bad times with my career and personal life. Behind all that are lessons that can make you stronger."

As to the ethnic discrimination that has recurrently hampered her career growth, Halle, a veteran at combating such bias, says, "I always have to rise above it. I can't go off like a raving lunatic even though my heart wants me to. I say, 'OK, take a deep breath,' and I realize that's the insidiousness of racism. People don't even know when they're being racists."

Regarding her "curse" of beauty that has often overshadowed her artistic talents, Berry points out, "Everybody tried to make believe that [my beauty] was the best thing about me. Then I realized no, that's not the best thing about me, that [it] could all be taken away tomorrow and I'd still have all the gifts that I have on the inside."

TIME LINE

1966 Born in Cleveland, Ohio, on August 14, the second of two children of a white mother and a black father

1970 Father abandons household for the first time; mother supports the family as a psychiatric nurse

1976 Father reappears in the family life, but leaves permanently after a tumultuous year; Mrs. Berry and her daughters move to Oakwood Village, a Cleveland suburb

1984 Graduates from Bedford High School

1985 Wins Miss Teen Ohio beauty pageant and Miss Teen All-American pageant; later a runner-up in the Miss USA and the Miss World pageants

1986 Quits Cleveland's Cuyahoga Community College; moves to Chicago to become a model and actor

1989 Relocates to New York City, where she is cast in the short-lived TV sitcom _Living Dolls_; diagnosed with diabetes

1991 Appears in the films _Jungle Fever_ (Universal), _Strictly Business_ (Warner Bros.), and _The Last Boy Scout_ (Warner Bros.)

1992 Featured in the movie _Boomerang_ (Paramount), stars in the miniseries _Queen_ (CBS-TV); meets Atlanta Braves baseball star David Justice; chosen as one of the most beautiful people in the world by _People_ and _Us_ magazines, the first of such media tributes

1993 Weds David Justice in Atlanta on January 1; appears in the films _CB4_ (Universal), _Father Hood_ (Buena Vista), and _The Program_ (Buena Vista)

1994 Featured in the big-screen release _The Flintstones_ (Universal)

1995 Costars in the made-for-cable entry _Solomon & Sheba_ (Showtime) and the theatrical release _Losing Isaiah_ (Paramount)

1996 Appears in _Executive Action_ (Warner Bros); has the title role in _The Rich Man's Wife_ (Paramount); plays a cameo in _Girl 6_ (Fox Searchlight); headlines _Race the Sun_ (Buena Vista); divorces David Justice and subsequently contemplates suicide; signed as spokesperson for Revlon Cosmetics

1997 Has colead in *B*A*P*S* (New Line Cinema); meets singer Eric Benét

1998 Appears in *Bulworth* (Twentieth Century Fox), *The Wedding* (ABC-TV), and *Why Do Fools Fall in Love?* (Warner Bros.)

1999 Executive produces and stars in the made-for-cable feature *Introducing Dorothy Dandridge* (HBO); wins the NAACP Image Award for Entertainer of the Year as well an Emmy and Golden Globe Award; announces engagement to Eric Benét

2000 Wins an Emmy and Golden Globe Award for *Introducing Dorothy Dandridge*; involved in an auto accident in Los Angeles—fined $13,500, placed on probation for three years, and required to perform 200 hours of community service; has colead in *X-Men* (Twentieth Century Fox)

2001 Marries Eric Benét on January 1 in southern California; adopts his daughter India; appears in *Swordfish* (Warner Bros) and *Monster's Ball* (Lions Gate)

2002 Wins several industry prizes for *Monster's Ball*, including Best Actress Academy Award; costars in the James Bond entry *Die Another Day* (MGM); rumors of problems in her marriage to Eric Benét

2003 Appears in *X-2: X-Men United* (Twentieth Century Fox) and *Gothika* (Warner Bros.); officially separates from Eric Benét

2004 Stars in *Catwoman* (Warner Bros.); in production for several upcoming feature films: *The Set-Up*, *Nappily Ever After*, *The Guide*, and *Robots*; files for divorce from Eric Benét

HOW TO BECOME AN ACTOR

THE JOB

The imitation or basic development of a character for presentation to an audience may seem like a glamorous and fairly easy job. In reality, it is demanding, tiring work that requires a special talent.

An actor must first find an available part in some upcoming production. This may be in a comedy, drama, musical, or opera. Then, having read and studied the part, the actor must audition before the director and other people who have control of the production. This requirement is often waived for established artists. In film and television, actors must also complete screen tests, which are scenes recorded on film, at times performed with other actors, which are later viewed by the director and producer of the film.

If selected for the part, the actor must spend hundreds of hours in rehearsal and must memorize many lines and cues. This is especially true in live theater; in film and television actors may spend less time in rehearsal and sometimes improvise their lines before the camera, often performing several attempts, or "takes," before the director is satisfied. Television actors often take advantage of TelePrompTers, which scroll lines on a screen in front of performing actors. Radio actors generally read from a script, and therefore their rehearsal times are usually shorter.

In addition to such mechanical duties, the actor must determine the essence of the character he or she is auditioning for, and the relation of that character to the overall scheme of the production. Radio actors must be especially skilled in expressing character and emotion through voice alone. In many film and theater roles actors must also sing and dance and spend additional time rehearsing songs and perfecting choreography. Certain roles require actors to perform various stunts, some of which can be quite dangerous. Specially trained performers usually complete these stunts. Others work as stand-ins or body doubles. These actors are chosen for specific features and appear on film in place of the lead actor;

this is often the case in films requiring nude or seminude scenes. Many television programs, such as game shows, also feature models, who generally assist the host of the program.

Actors in the theater may perform the same part many times a week for weeks, months, and sometimes years. This allows them to develop the role, but it can also become tedious. Actors in films may spend several weeks involved in a production, which often takes place on location (that is, in different parts of the world). Television actors involved in a series, such as a soap opera or a situation comedy, also may play the same role for years, generally in 13-week cycles. For these actors, however, their lines change from week to week and even from day to day, and much time is spent rehearsing their new lines.

While studying and perfecting their craft, many actors work as extras, the nonspeaking characters who appear in the background on screen or stage. Many actors also continue training throughout their careers. A great deal of an actor's time is spent attending auditions.

REQUIREMENTS

High School

There are no minimum educational requirements to become an actor. However, at least a high school diploma is recommended. In high school English classes you will learn about the history of drama and the development of strong characters. Take music classes to help you develop your voice and ability to read music, which are valuable skills for any actor, even those who do not perform many musical roles.

Postsecondary Training

As acting becomes more and more involved with the various facets of society, a college degree will become more important to those who hope to have an acting career. An actor who has completed a liberal arts program is thought to be more capable of understanding the wide variety of roles that are available. Therefore, it is strongly recommended that aspiring actors complete at least a bachelor's degree program in theater or the dramatic arts. In addition, graduate degrees in the fine arts or in drama are nearly always required should the individual decide to teach dramatic arts.

College can also provide acting experience for the hopeful actor. More than 500 colleges and universities throughout the country offer dramatic arts programs and present theatrical performances. Actors and directors recommend that those interested in acting gain as much experience as possible through acting in high school and college plays or in those offered by community groups. Training beyond college is recommended, especially for actors interested in entering the theater. Joining acting workshops, such as the Actors Studio, can often be highly competitive.

Other Requirements

Prospective actors will be required not only to have a great talent for acting but also a great determination to succeed in the theater and motion pictures. They must be able to memorize hundreds of lines and should have a good speaking voice. The ability to sing and dance is important for increasing the opportunities for the young actor. Almost all actors are required to audition for a part before they receive the role. In film and television actors will generally complete screen tests to see how they appear on film. In all fields of acting, a love of performing is a must. It might take many years for an actor to achieve any success, if they achieve it at all.

Performers on Broadway stages must be members of the Actors' Equity Association before being cast. While union membership may not always be required, many actors find it advantageous to belong to a union that covers their particular field of performing arts. These organizations include the Actors' Equity Association (stage), Screen Actors Guild or Screen Extras Guild (motion pictures and television films), or American Federation of Television and Radio Artists (TV, recording, and radio). In addition, some actors may benefit from membership in the American Guild of Variety Artists (nightclubs and so on), American Guild of Musical Artists (opera and ballet), or organizations such as the Hebrew Actors Union or Italian Actors Union for productions in those languages.

EXPLORING

The best way to explore this career is to participate in school or local theater productions. Even working on the props or lighting crew will provide insight into the field.

Also, attend as many dramatic productions as possible and try to talk with people who either are currently in the theater or have been at one time. They can offer advice to individuals interested in a career in the theater.

There are many books about acting that concern not only how to perform, but also the nature of the work, its offerings, advantages, and disadvantages.

EMPLOYERS

Motion pictures, television, and the stage are the largest fields of employment for actors, with television commercials representing as much as 60 percent of all acting jobs. Most of the opportunities for employment in these fields are either in Los Angeles or in New York. On the stage, even the road shows often have their beginning in New York, with the selection of actors conducted there along with rehearsals. However, nearly every city and most communities present local and regional theater productions.

As cable television networks continue to produce more and more of their own programs and films, they will become a major provider of employment for actors. Home video will also continue to create new acting jobs, as will the music video business.

The lowest numbers of actors are employed for stage work. In addition to Broadway shows and regional theater, there are employment opportunities for stage actors in summer stock, at resorts, and on cruise ships.

STARTING OUT

Probably the best way to enter acting is to start with high school, local, or college productions and gain as much experience as possible on that level. Very rarely is an inexperienced actor given an opportunity to perform onstage or in a film in New York or Hollywood. The field is extremely difficult to enter; the more experience and ability beginners have, however, the greater the possibilities for entrance.

Those venturing to New York or Hollywood are encouraged first to have enough money to support themselves during the long waiting and searching period normally required before a job is found. Most will list themselves with a casting agency that will help them find a part as an extra or a bit player, either in theater or film. These agencies keep names on file along with photographs and a description of the individual's features and experience, and if a part comes along that may be suitable, they contact that person. Very often, however, names are added to their lists only when the number of people in a particular physical category is low. For instance, the agency may not have enough athletic young women on its roster, and if the applicant happens to fit this description, her name is added.

ADVANCEMENT

New actors will normally start with bit parts and will have only a few lines to speak, if any. The normal progression would then be landing larger supporting roles and then, in the case of theater, possibly a role as an understudy for one of the main actors. The understudy usually has an opportunity to fill in should the main actor be unable to give a performance. Many film and television actors get their start in commercials or by appearing in government and commercially sponsored public service announcements, films, and programs. Other actors join the afternoon soap operas and continue on to evening programs. Many actors also have started in on-camera roles such as presenting the weather segment of a local news program. Once an actor has gained experience, he or she may go on to play stronger supporting roles or even leading roles in stage, television, or film productions. From there, an actor may go on to stardom. Only a very small number of actors ever reach that pinnacle, however.

Some actors eventually go into other, related occupations and become drama coaches, drama teachers, producers, stage directors, motion picture directors, television directors, radio directors, stage managers, casting directors, or artist and repertoire managers. Others may combine one or more of these functions while continuing their careers.

EARNINGS

The wage scale for actors is largely controlled through bargaining agreements reached by various unions in negotiations with producers. These agreements normally control the minimum salaries, hours of work permitted per week, and other conditions of employment. In addition, each artist enters into a separate contract that may provide for higher salaries.

In 2002 the minimum daily salary of any member of the Screen Actors Guild (SAG) in a speaking role was $655, or $2,272 for a five-day workweek. Motion picture actors may also receive additional payments known as residuals as part of their guaranteed salary. Many motion picture actors receive residuals whenever films, TV shows, and TV commercials in which they appear are rerun, sold for

TV exhibition, or put on DVD. Residuals often exceed the actor's original salary and account for about one-third of all actors' income.

A wide range of earnings can be seen when reviewing the Actors' Equity Association's *Annual Report 2000,* which includes a breakdown of average weekly salaries by contract type and location. According to the report, for example, those in off-Broadway productions earned an average weekly salary of $642 during the 1999–2000 season. Other average weekly earnings for the same period include: San Francisco Bay Area theater, $329; New England area theater, $236; Walt Disney World in Orlando, Florida, $704; and Chicago area theater, $406. The report concludes that the median weekly salary for all contract areas is $457. Most actors do not work 52 weeks per year; in fact, the report notes that of the 38,013 members in good standing only 16,976 were employed. The majority of those employed, approximately 12,000, had annual earnings ranging from $1 to $15,000.

According to the U.S. Department of Labor, the median yearly earning of all actors was $25,920 in 2000. The department also reported the lowest paid 10 percent earned less than $12,700 annually, while the highest paid 10 percent made more than $93,620.

The annual earnings of persons in television and movies are affected by frequent periods of unemployment. According to SAG, most of its members earn less than $7,500 a year from acting jobs. Unions offer health, welfare, and pension funds for members working more than a set number of weeks a year. Some actors are eligible for paid vacation and sick time, depending on the work contract.

In all fields, well-known actors have salary rates above the minimums, and the salaries of the few top stars are many times higher. Actors in television series may earn tens of thousands of dollars per week, while a few may earn as much as $1 million or more per week. Salaries for these actors vary considerably and are negotiated individually. In film, top stars may earn as much as $20 million per film, and, after receiving a percentage of the gross earned by the film, these stars can earn far, far more.

Until recent years, female film stars tended to earn lower salaries than their male counterparts; stars such as Julia Roberts, Jodie Foster, Halle Berry, and others have started to reverse that trend. The average annual earnings for all motion picture actors, however, are usually low for all but the best-known performers because of the periods of unemployment.

WORK ENVIRONMENT

Actors work under varying conditions. Those employed in motion pictures may work in air-conditioned studios one week and be on location in a hot desert the next.

Those in stage productions perform under all types of conditions. The number of hours employed per day or week varies, as does the number of weeks employed per year. Stage actors normally perform eight shows per week with any additional performances paid for as overtime. The basic workweek after the show opens is about 36 hours unless major changes in the play are needed. The number of hours worked per week is considerably more before the opening because of rehearsals. Evening work is a natural part of a stage actor's life. Rehearsals often are held at night and over holidays and weekends. If the play goes on the road, much traveling will be involved.

A number of actors cannot receive unemployment compensation when they are waiting for their next part, primarily because they have not worked enough to meet the minimum eligibility requirements for compensation. Sick leaves and paid vacations are not usually available to the actor. However, union actors who earn the minimum qualifications now receive full medical and health insurance under all the actors' unions. Those who earn health-plan benefits for 10 years become eligible for a pension upon retirement. The acting field is very uncertain. Aspirants never know whether they will be able to get into the profession, and, once in, there are uncertainties as to whether the show will be well-received and, if not, whether the actors' talent can survive a bad show.

OUTLOOK

Employment in acting is expected to grow faster than the average through 2010, according to the U.S. Department of Labor. There are a number of reasons for this. The growth of satellite and cable television in the past decade has created a demand for more actors, especially as the cable networks produce more and more of their own programs and films. The rise of home video and DVD has also created new acting jobs, as more and more films are made strictly for the home-video market. Many resorts built in the 1980s and 1990s present their own theatrical productions, providing more job opportunities for actors. Jobs in theater, however, face pressure as the cost of mounting a production rises and as many nonprofit and smaller theaters lose their funding.

Despite the growth in opportunities, there are many more actors than there are roles, and this is likely to remain true for years to come. This is true in all areas of the arts, including radio, television, motion pictures, and theater, and even those who are employed are normally employed during only a small portion of the year. Many actors must supplement their income by working at other jobs, such as secretaries, waiters, or taxi drivers, for example. Almost all performers are members of more than one union in order to take advantage of various opportunities as they become available.

It should be recognized that of the 105,000 or so actors in the United States today, an average of only about 16,000 are employed at any one time. Of these, few are able to support themselves on their earnings from acting, and fewer still will ever achieve stardom. Most actors work for many years before becoming known, and most of these do not rise above supporting roles. The vast majority of actors, meanwhile, are still looking for the right break. There are many more applicants in all areas than there are positions. As with most careers in the arts, people enter this career out of a genuine love of acting.

TO LEARN MORE ABOUT ACTORS

BOOKS

Bruder, Melissa. *A Practical Handbook for the Actor.* New York: Vintage, 1986.

Lee, Robert L. *Everything about Theater!: The Guidebook of Theater Fundamentals.* Colorado Springs, Colo.: Meriwether, 1996.

Quinlan, Kathryn A. *Actor.* Mankato, Minn.: Capstone Press, 1998.

Stevens, Chambers. *Magnificent Monologues for Kids.* South Pasadena, Calif.: Sandcastle, 1999.

WEBSITES AND ORGANIZATIONS

The Actors' Equity Association is a professional union for actors in theater and "live" industrial productions, stage managers, some directors, and choreographers.

Actors' Equity Association

165 West 46th Street

New York, NY 10036

Tel: 212-869-8530

E-mail: info@actorsequity.org

http://www.actorsequity.org

This union represents television and radio performers, including actors, announcers, dancers, disc jockeys, newspersons, singers, specialty acts, sportscasters, and stunt persons.

American Federation of Television and Radio Artists

260 Madison Avenue

New York, NY 10016-2402

Tel: 212-532-0800

E-mail: aftra@aftra.com

http://www.aftra.com

A directory of theatrical programs may be purchased from NAST. For answers to a number of frequently asked questions concerning education, visit the NAST website.

National Association of Schools of Theater (NAST)

11250 Roger Bacon Drive, Suite 21

Reston, VA 20190

Tel: 703-437-0700

E-mail: info@arts-accredit.org

http://www.arts-accredit.org/nast

The Screen Actors Guild (SAG) provides general information on actors, directors, and producers. Visit the SAG website for more information.

Screen Actors Guild (SAG)

5757 Wilshire Boulevard

Los Angeles, CA 90036-3600

Tel: 323-954-1600

http://www.sag.com

For information about opportunities in not-for-profit theaters, contact

Theatre Communications Group

355 Lexington Avenue

New York, NY 10017

Tel: 212-697-5230

E-mail: tcg@tcg.org

http://www.tcg.org

This site has information for beginners on acting and the acting business.

Acting Workshop On-Line

http://www.redbirdstudio.com/AWOL/acting2.html

TO LEARN MORE ABOUT HALLE BERRY

BOOKS

Bogle, Donald. *Dorothy Dandridge*. New York: St. Martin's, 1997.

Ebert, Roger. *Roger Ebert's Movie Yearbook 2003*. Kansas City, Kans.: Andrews McMeel, 2002.

Editors. *Current Biography Yearbook 1999*. Bronx, N.Y.: H. W. Wilson, 2000.

Farley, Christopher John. *Introducing Halle Berry*. New York: Pocket Books, 2002.

Kenyatta, Kelly. *Red Hot Halle: The Story of an American Best Actress*. Chicago: Star Books, 2003.

Naden, Corinne J. and Rose Blue. *Halle Berry*. Philadelphia: Chelsea House, 2002.*

O'Brien, Daniel. *Halle Berry*. London: Reynolds & Hearn, 2003.

Parish, James Robert. *Today's Black Hollywood*. New York: Kensington, 1995.

Parish, James Robert, and Allan Taylor, eds. *The Encyclopedia of Ethnic Groups in Hollywood*. New York: Facts On File, 2002.

Phelps, Shirelle, ed. *Contemporary Black Biography*, Vol. 19. Detroit: Gale, 1999.

Sanello, Frank. *Halle Berry: A Stormy Life*. London: Virgin Books, 2003.

* Young Adult book

MAGAZINES

Berry, Halle. "The Year That Changed My Life." *Essence*, December 2002.

Clehane, Diane. "Halle's Comet." *Biography*, January 2001.

Ely, Suzanne. "Halle Berry: Her Secret Source of Strength." *Redbook*, March 2003.

Grobel, Larry. "Glory, Glory Halle-lujah." *Movieline*, December/January 2002.

_____. "Halle Berry." *Playboy*, January 2003.

Hensley, Dennis. "Ripe Berry." *Movieline*, August 1999.

Sessums, Kevin. "The 9 Lives of Halle Berry." *Elle*, October 2003.

Van Meter, Jonathan. "Solid Gold." *Vogue*, December 2002.

WEBSITES

Halle Berry Online Shrine

http://www.online-shrine.com/berry/

Hallewood: The Official Halle Berry Website

http://www.hallewood.com

Internet Movie Database

http://www.imdb.com

* * *

American Diabetes Association

http://www.diabetes.org

National Coalition Against Domestic Violence

http://www.ncadv.org

National Domestic Violence Hotline

http://www.ndvh.org

Violence Against Women Online Resources

http://www.vaw.umn.edu/library

INDEX

Page numbers in *italics* indicate illustrations.

A

actors
  career advancement
    102–103
  career beginning 101–102
  career exploration 100
  educational requirements
    97–99
  employers 100–101
  employment outlook
    107–108
  job description 95–97
  other requirements 99–100
  salaries of 103–105
  work environment
    105–106
Aguilera, Christina 4
Amen (TV series) 25
Atlanta Braves 31, 51

B

B*A*P*S (film) *55,* 56
Beatty, Warren 57–58, *58*
Bedford High School 13
Benét, Eric 68–69, *69,* 70–71,
  77, 79, 83–84
Benét, India (daughter) 69–70,
  84
Berry, Halle
  abuse by father 3, 8, 10–11,
    53, 67
  and therapy 10, 37, 50
  as actor 14–15, 19, 21–23,
    25–30, 34, *35,* 36–37, *39,*
    40, *41,* 43–44, *44,* 45–46,
    49–50, 55–56, *58,* 59,
    66–68, 70, 73–74, *74,* 75,
    77–78, *78,* 79–85, *85,*
    86–87, *87,* 88

Berry, Halle *(continued)*
  as beauty pageant contestant
    15, *16,* 17–18, 55
  as model 15, *16,* 18–19,
    21–23, *23,* 25–27, 54
  as producer 65–67, 86
  as role model 1, 38–40, 43,
    54–55, 79
  automobile accident of
    70–73
  awards and award
    nominations 1, *2,* 4, *9,*
    36, 42–43, 57–58, 68, 79,
    82–83, *87,* 88
  birth of 7
  career as journalist 17–18
  childhood 3, 7–8, 10–12
  diabetes of, 3, 24–25
  discrimination against 3–5,
    11–14, 19, 88
  divorce of parents 8, 10
  domestic abuse 27–28
  education 11–15, 17–18
  film work 1, 26–30, 37–39,
    39, 40, *41,* 42–43, *44,*
    44–45, *45,* 46, *55,* 55–58,
    58, 59, 70, 73, *74,* 74–75,
    77–78, *78,* 79–80, *80,*
    81–85, *85,* 86–88
  health of 3, 23–25, 37,
    70–72, 85–86
  homes of 10–11, 18, 21,
    31–32

  marriages and divorces
    31–32, 47, 49–52, *52,*
    53–54, 77, 83–84
  personal goals 13–14, 43,
    84, 88–89
  physical characteristics of
    4, 22, *23,* 34, 88–89
  role models for 1, 7, 12, 56,
    61
  romantic relationships
    27–28, 30–32, *68,*
    68–70
  talks about herself 8,
    10–14, 17, 22, 24–25, 27,
    34, 37–38, 43, 46, 50–51,
    53–54, 67, 72–73, 79,
    83–84, 88–89
  television work 21–23, 25,
    34, *35,* 36, 42–43, 56–57,
    65–66, *66,* 67–68
  theater work 14
Berry, Heidi (sister) 8, 10–11
Berry, Jerome (father) 3, 7–8,
    10, 53, 67
Berry, Judith Hawkins
    (mother) 3, 7–8, *9,* 10–12, 14,
    18–19, 44, 54
Bogle Donald, 65
Boomerang (film) 29–30
Boyle Peter, 81
Brandauer, Klaus Maria *66*
Brando, Marlon 79
Bratt, Benjamin 86

Bright Road (film) 64
Bulworth (film) 57–58, *58*

C

Cardosa, Patricia 86–87
Carey, Mariah 5
Carmen Jones (film) 61, 64
Catwoman (film) 86
CB4 (film) 37
Charlie's Angels (TV series) 21
Cirrincione, Vincent 19, 21, 54, 65
Cleveland City Hospital 7, 63
Combs, Sean "P. Diddy" 81
Coolidge, Martha 66
The Country Girl (film) 61
Crowe, Russell 82–83
Cruz, Penelope 86
Curry, Ann 5
Cuyahoga Community College 17

D

Dandridge, Dorothy 7, 59, 61, *62*, 63–68
Dandridge, Ruby 63
Dandridge, Vivian 63
Daniels, Lee 81
Davidson, Tommy 28
Days of Our Lives (TV series) 21
De Niro, Robert 79
The Decks Ran Red (film) 64
Dench, Judi 1

Desselle, Natalie *55*
Diabetes 3, 24–25
Die Another Day (film) 84–85, 87
Diesel, Vin 5
A Different World (TV series) 25
Dorothy Dandridge: A Portrait in Black (book) 65
Downey, Robert, Jr. 86
Dutton, Charles S. 86

E

The Effect of Gamma Rays on Man-in-the-Moon Marigolds (play) 14
Epps, Omar 38
Erman, John 34
Executive Decision (film) 43, *44*

F

Father Hood (film) 37
The Flintstones (film) 38–39, *39*, 40
The Flintstones (TV series) 38
Foster, Marc 80, 83

G

Girl 6 (film) 45
Givens, Robin 29–30
Glover, Danny 36
Goodman, John 38
Gothika (film) *85*, 86

The Guide (film) 87
Gyllenhaal, Stephen 40, 42

H

Haley, Alex 33–34
Harpo Productions 57
Hooks, Kevin 28
Hope, Bob 15
Horne, Lena 63–64
Houston, Whitney 65

I

Indecent Proposal (film) 46
Introducing Dorothy Dandridge
(TV film) 59, *66,* 66–68, 70, 77

J

Jackman, Hugh 78
Jackson, Samuel J. 26
Jeffries, Marc John *41*
Jones, Amy Holden 46
Jones, Tommy Lee 79
Jordan, Eric Benét. *See* Benét,
Eric
Jungle Fever (film) 25–28, 40
Justice, David 30–32, 47, 49–51,
52, 53–54, 77
Juvenile Diabetes Foundation
25

K

Kelly, Grace 61
Keys, Alicia 5

Kidd, Jason 5
Kidman, Nicole 1
Knots Landing (TV series) 25

L

Lange, Jessica 42
The Last Boy Scout (film) 29
Ledger, Heath 81
Lee, Spike 25–26, 40, 45
Living Dolls (TV series) 22–23
Lord & Taylor Department
Store 19
Losing Isaiah (film) 40, *41,* 42
Lumbly, Carl 57

M

Marshall Field's Department
Store 19
Marvel Comics 73
McDonald, Christopher *45*
Menace II Society (film) 38
Mills, Earl 65
Miss Teen All-American beauty
pageant 15
Miss Teen Ohio beauty pageant
15
Miss USA beauty pageant 15, *16*
Miss World beauty pageant 17
Mitchell, Kay 18
Monster's Ball (film) 1, 79–80,
80, 81–82, 84
Moore, Demi 46
Moranis, Rick 38

Murphy, Eddie 29–30
Mystic Pizza (film) 46

N
NAACP. *See* National
  Association for the
  Advancement of Colored
  People
Nappily Ever After (film) 86–87
National Association for the
  Advancement of Colored
  People (NAACP) 36, 42–43,
  57–58, 68, 79
Nava, Gregory 59
Nicholas, Harold 63
NYPD Blues (TV series) 43

O
Oakley, Charles 27
O'Donnell, Rosie 38–39

P
Penn, Sean 79
Perkins, Elizabeth 38
Phillips, Joseph C. 28
Poitier, Sidney 64
Porgy and Bess (film) 64
The Program (film) 38

Q
Queen (book) 33
Queen (TV miniseries) 34, *35*,
  36–37

R
Race the Sun (film) 44–45
Raythata, Heta 71–73
Reeves, Keanu 5
Revlon Cosmetics 4, 54
The Rich Man's Wife (film) *45*,
  45–46
Robots (film) 88
Rock, Chris 37
Roots (book) 33
Roots (TV miniseries) 33
Russell, Kurt 43

S
Sciorra, Annabella 25
Seagal, Steven 43
The Set-Up (film) 86
Silver, Joel 29, 43, 78, 86
Sims, Yvonne Nichols 12–13
Singer, Bryan 73
Smits, Jimmy 42–43
Snipes, Wesley 25, 27
Solomon & Sheba (TV film)
  42–43
Spacek, Sissy 1
Spelling, Aaron 22
"Spend My Life With You"
  (song) 69
Spielberg, Steven 38
Sports Center (TV series) 49
Stauff, Tami 69
Stevens, David 33
Stone, Oliver 79

Stone, Sharon 39, 86
Strictly Business (film) 28
Swordfish (film) 77–78, 78, 79

T
Tamahori, Lee 87
Tarzan's Peril (film) 64
Thal, Eric 57
Thornton, Billy Bob 80, 81–82
Townsend, Robert 56
Travolta, John 78, 78
True to Myself (recording) 69

W
Walters, Barbara 53
Wayans, Damon 29
The Wedding (TV film) 56–57
West, Dorothy 57

Why Do Fools Fall in Love?
  (film) 59
Williams, Christopher 27
Williams, Wendie 66
Willis, Bruce 29
Winfrey, Oprah 56–57
The Wizard of Oz (film) 15
Woods, Tiger 4

X
X-Men (film) 70, 73, 74, 74–75,
  77, 86
X-Men 2: X-Men United (film)
  74–75, 86

Z
Zellweger, Renée 1

ABOUT THE AUTHOR

James Robert Parish, a former entertainment reporter, publicist, and book series editor, is the author of numerous biographies and reference books about the entertainment industry, including *Stephen King: Author, Tom Hanks: Actor, Steven Spielberg: Filmmaker, Whitney Houston, The Hollywood Book of Love, Hollywood Divas, Hollywood Bad Boys, The Encyclopedia of Ethnic Groups in Hollywood, Jet Li, Jason Biggs, Gus Van Sant, The Hollywood Book of Death, Whoopi Goldberg, Rosie O'Donnell's Story, The Unofficial "Murder, She Wrote" Casebook, Today's Black Hollywood, Let's Talk! America's Favorite TV Talk Show Hosts, Black Action Pictures, Liza Minnelli, The Elvis Presley Scrapbook,* and *Hollywood's Great Love Teams.*

Mr. Parish is a frequent on-camera interviewee on cable and network TV for documentaries on the performing arts both in the United States and in the United Kingdom. He resides in Studio City, California.